Pageant of Words

Poems of Reflection on Life, Imagination and Renewal

Agustin Medina

ISBN Paperback: 978-1-964422-21-3

ISBN Hardback: 978-1-964422-22-0

*Dedicated to my wife of over fifty years, Sadie, to our children Chris,
Alicia and Daniel, and to their own families.
Amor Vincit Omnia.*

ABOUT THE AUTHOR

Agustin (Augie) Medina is a semi-retired Latino attorney who has practiced law in the area of business litigation for 47 years. He has degrees from UCLA and Stanford University and is a Vietnam Era military veteran. Outside of the law, his passions are music (he plays keyboard, guitar and ukulele and loves blues and doo-wop music equally with classical music and opera), literature (Dante's <u>The Divine Comedy</u> and Cervantes' <u>Don Quixote</u> are his favorite pieces of literature) and extreme outdoors activities (mountain climbing, rock climbing and canyoneering). He maintains that, of all written forms of expression, poetry provides the greatest economy of scale for saying something in compelling, memorable fashion.

CONTENTS

PREFACE

This little volume is a compilation of my poetry. I began writing poetry relatively late in life, around the age of 50. Although I've taken a few poetry workshops, I've never entered into a formal program of study of poetry, and I do not have a degree in literature. Poetry, for me, as I'm sure for many others, is a vehicle for personal expression. I write mainly in free verse style, and my subjects range from the political to the personal. I have organized the poems roughly according to subject or theme.

Although I've had a number of my poems published (two in an anthology and the rest on online sites), this is my first published collection. As with most poetry books, I do not expect anything beyond a limited readership. I have in mind as a target audience principally my own descendants. For those descendants who open the covers of this volume, they will find something of what I was and what I thought -expressed in verse- in my mature years. For all others who might dip into this collection, my hope is that they can relate to these poems as expressions of their own reflections and experiences.

NATURE

TENDER FINGERS OF NIGHT

The day yearns for night
My long day's journey blends into dusk
I walk into sunsets of red and orange

From the dark
I look up at the twinkling heavenly canvas
Speckled moonlight falls on the lake

I envy the swaying trees moved by warm winds
I hear cricket symphonies
Glens and rivers slow to listen

Passionate wild roses
Offer a whiff of Eden
I sense the longing of the lavender wildflowers
To be told "you are captivating, you are amazing"

The mosaic of gentle stones glide under my feet
The cosmos whispers that
Only divine love escapes from black holes

These are pillows for the heart
As I rest on the earth
Surrounded by a cathedral of peaks
In a canyon of glory cut by flowing waters of grace

These are deeper than reality
I cannot really know them
I can only dream

GUANAJUATO SUNRISE

I was there before dawn's bleary eyes opened
to reveal the sun lifting from night's repose
I felt glorious seated in my little canoe
watching the palm trees along the bank
sprout a glow of orange

The river rippled gently underneath
a refrain to the call of the unfolding sunrise
the river thanking Helios for another day
in the land of the Aztecs
land of an orange cast

The outstretched warmth of the sun
coaxed fragrance from the palms
calling to memory
the same fragrance
that perfumes my hometown's air
where sister palms grow
and memories fuse

IN NATURE'S TEMPLE

I bask in my warm, quiet evening years:
breathe easy-*nefesh*-let the mind unfurl
without fear of societal judgment and its boxes
I am at ease about what is happening around me

I have returned to basics
The outdoors is life-affirming
In the morning, I stroll on a carpet of pinecones and leaves
under a thicket of Jeffrey Pines and Coastal Oak
I wade barefoot in the cool waters of a gentle stream

The wind befriends me
A temperate breeze calms my thoughts
I am content with nature at my reach

Come night time, a mountain moon is my light
A volume of verse is my companion
I hear the song of the valley sweeping down
along its V-shaped contour ending with a plagal cadence
I want for nothing in the temple of nature

EXALTED CANYON

Eons of swift water massaged to a jagged finish
the rugged fissure punched into the mountain

Boulders sweep its majestic course
detained in awkward postures along the way

The sun hovers over the canyon rim and drops its warmth
while rocks crumble from granite walls

Trees in the watercourse bombard the eye
sprinkled over a carpet of rich green, promiscuous growth

Winds whip the leaves, sounding like sizzling bacon
The canyon gods exult over their creation

THE WILD CREEK

Snowmelt from the white mountain-top
The murmur of the flowing icy waters captivates me
like the Sirens that lured Odysseus' men

The water gently tumbles over pebbles, twigs and sand
then suddenly accelerates as it spills over granite boulders
into whirling pools that scour the bottom of the wild creek

The wild creek's banks are adorned with gnarled trees,
rich green flora, and piles of boulders, large and small

I drop into the creek bed along a steep, mossy incline
to gaze at the raw beauty of this bed of rocks and sand
that through millennia has carved the canyon through which it runs

As I stand and enjoy the sylvan stillness
I marvel that this creek and canyon were here
before the Babylonian Captivity

The journey of the water is much like life
Swift, slow, ebbing then flowing, whirling and then calm,
not knowing what awaits downstream

LOVE IN THE FOREST

She found him in the remotest part of the forest
A magnificent tree in a sylvan paradise
Verdant, lush, redolent of nature's fragrance

Parched and needing revival
She lay in his shade and
Tasted his fruit well into the comforting night

The stars throbbed overhead and penetrated
The dark where she lay
The span of his branches protected her
From the chill of their outdoor bed chamber

Impregnated, she rooted in the ground beside him
As she grew over the years, her branches intertwined with his
Until two trees became one
That is the way of love in the forest

THE POETRY TRAIL

The light brown dusty trail
Affords me contentment
Sage, paintbrush and miner's lettuce
Adorn its edge

From the trail I gaze at
Distant ridges and peaks
That multiply toward the horizon

Lizards flash across my path
Reminders of the abundance of life out here
A rattlesnake vibrates its tail
To warn that nature must be respected

The sun beats down from its blue canvas
Heating the terrain and sucking its moisture
Tit for tat, the hydrologic cycle

The trail has taken me to the bottom of a small peak
A shaded glen to the side affords a place to recover from the exertion
I munch a snack and open my poetry volume
The trail was meant for poetry and poetry for the trail

UNPREPARED

That day I hoisted my body up the rugged mountain
Shivering wildly as my paper-thin jacket surrendered
to the icy breath of the alpine wind
At the summit, I was alone; no one to share my misery with

On my descent, I crossed a swift stream barefoot
No protection for the flesh of my feet
I regretted coming out to challenge nature unprepared

RELATIONSHIPS

FIRE WAS NEVER ENOUGH

Fire was never enough
In the days we made love in the snow

Bare bottoms bathed in the moonlight
Limbs sinking through airy crystals
A measured iambic rhythm
As befits a poet lover

Some say love is more fashionable
In the warmth
But no fashion for us
My lover was cold as ice
A natural in our bed of snow
Our talk would fill the frigid night
Icy nothings in our breaths' vapors

It was a glorious time—
Then
Society lured us into its polite fabric
No more love in the virgin snow

I often wonder where she is today
And how she remembers those times
Most of all, I wonder why
She would always insist
"Fire is never enough"

THE TRUEST OF FRIENDS

Three close friends had a curious question
How many allotted heartbeats did each have?
Turns out two of them had quite a few more than the third
Thanks to free-flowing arteries based on clean living
But they sought equality of life and so
They summed their heartbeats and divided by three

Now each had equal time on earth
They would pass on the same day

There was never a greater friendship

A FAILED RELATIONSHIP

An Apollo-like hunk on my dating app agreed to meet
He turned out a smooth talker and buffed to a "V"
I decided to go for it and encouraged come-hither outpourings
He WhatsApp'd me sweet messages
Bought me mint tea lattes
Took my hand down Melrose Ave.
Turned me into his Queen Dido

But it ended quickly
He said he wasn't ready
'Ready for what?'
'For you. You're too much
For me right now'
I thought I was barely enough
He didn't elaborate
Just walked off

Was that bad karma or what?
I envisioned Dido's funeral pyre
But I calmed my overdramatic psyche
And called my therapist
She said she could help
But her hourly rate had gone up
Cudgeled by a Ph.D

I retreated to my gated condo
Where I wanted the gate to stay open
As a symbol that I was not trapped
But the guard said no

I got into my crying clothes
And wept until dawn
Why isn't heartache less painful
In this digital and entitled era?
We shouldn't have to suffer as much as before the internet

Painless relationships might
Improve the human condition
--Or maybe negate its essence--
I'm glad I don't have to decide
I might decide wrong

WHY I'M GRATEFUL

I am glad my friend that I was not born
Dante, Cervantes, Dickens or Flaubert
Ovid, Neruda, Keats or Shakespeare
Nor Palestrina, Mozart, Beethoven or Schubert
Not Thorpe, Ruth, Ali, Palmer, Mays or Koufax
Not even Einstein, Newton, Galileo or LaPlace
Not Hegel, Kant, Hume or Descartes
Neither Rembrandt, Michelangelo, Rivera nor Picasso
Because then, I never would have had a life with my wife,
my children and grandchildren
These famous people had families
But none of them had mine.

TRYING TO IMPRESS

He told her
of mad adventures past;
that he had cooled his hands
in the fading twilight of the land of Oz;
that he had wandered along the Ionian shores
during the times of the ancient lights
looking for magic and resurgence
She said "What a crock!"

PENTATONIC MARRIAGE

It lasted five short years
Born of a bar stool meeting
And carried on a river of tears

High shiny leather boots
Tight ass skirt and
Rite Aid perfume

Was all it took
To get me to pop the question--
(Oh and a bottle of Mr. Daniel's finest
With a dozen Bud chasers)

Like someone once sang
'We was married in a fever,
Hotter'n a pepper sprout'

Busted on our wedding night
Charge was possession 10 grams
Didn't even get in one good snort,
I was like 'hot damn!'

She got five months in county
Had our first kid there-
Five pounds, five ounces-
Came while sittin' in a chair

On the outside, our five-hundred-square-foot
Rental unit was always filled with luckless friends
And non-stop party-hearty

One day, we said we'd had enough
Of one and each the other
So we went down to the courthouse
Filled out one of them free forms
Five dollars to file
And we were done
Five years of hardship
And very little fun

TWO DANCERS

The music had a tango beat
The two danced skillfully in mirth and laughter
Enamored of dance—no more and no less
He, a future priest
She, his fetching aunt
Stepping and twirling in glee
In a shanty in the back

The dance of innocence ended tragically that afternoon
Her husband coming upon the scene
Rendered crazed by the sight of his wife
Being gently led in rhythm
By the future priest

I heard the black shouts
Felt the air agitated by the torrent of rage
The ambient light turned dark by the surge of jealousy
Instigated by the perceived betrayal
Of a wife and a future priest

Raised off her dancer's feet by her auburn hair
And thrown through an open door
Onto the ground below a stately elm
She lay dazed, crumpled and shorn of dignity

The husband turned toxic to his very core
His face contorted by fiendish spasms
Poured out his wrath in a hail of angry fists
Onto the temperate face of the future priest
Too stunned to respond, the young man remained
Uncomprehending about the dangers of dance

In the brief time that violence
Stalked the floor of the shanty
Where happy dancing feet had trod just moments before
Family ties were rendered asunder
Into fragments too fragile to reconnect

What was the terrible alchemy
That converted an innocent scene of mirth into accusations of sin?
At the cost of family bonds
At the cost of the well-being of two dancers

The answer was beyond the grasp of a 10-year-old mind
Who had enjoyed just minutes before
The sight of dancers swaying to a tango beat

SPECIAL PEOPLE

LADY OF THE BOOKS

Oh, the things she read!
They only found out after she was dead
She had smorgasbord tastes
No book went to waste

Romances, histories, even light porn
Poetry and a 'how to' on the growing of corn
Math texts, travel guides and biographies
Books on cooking, wines and good cheese
Even Bach on counterpoint, would you believe?
Universal knowledge she wished to achieve

Books on the shelves and scattered on the floor
This was the scene when they walked through the door
A natural death but she had dressed to the nines
In full-length dress and jewelry that shined

In the curious way that things sometimes turn out
No one ever learned what she was about
But if you want and know where to look
You'll find her just known as Lady of the Books

TO MOTHER FOREVER

Last night, a candle flickered for you
It was a flame of remembrance
    For the days you graced my life
    For your guidance on how to be a woman
    For the beauty you passed to me
    For your willingness to impose discipline
    when the immature child did not know the good in it
    For giving me curiosity of mind and the exuberance to inquire
I daily breathe your spirit
You were as a comet in the heavens
    Bright and impactful while here
    But too short in duration of view
May the raiment of the heavens keep you
    in eternal peace
Eternal love I give to you.

To My Wife on Her 70th Birthday. You are

SO RARE

These words are a small token
of gratitude for the love, light and laughter you have given me
over the decades of our life together

This poem begins way back
when you unseated the heart of a teenage boy
with a beauty and grace beyond any accounting of it

Your heart always seemed full of the bloom of sunflowers
with ready exuberance for the well-being of others
You displayed the overwhelming power of a gentle smile
Over time, our daily rhythms became interlocked
and two people became one

Three children whose heartbeats began inside you
gave us years of diapers, skinned knees
and dealing with adolescent pangs
Then graduations, and finally witnessing our children
taking the very marital vows we took
To begin the circle anew

From high school sweethearts to grandparents
Now seems as the duration of a firefly's light
Bright, swift, yet with more light to come

You've always given the fullest form of love
Enriching the lives of all who've known it
You are
So rare

LIFE

THE PHYSICIST

He walked in quietly, looking forlorn, defeated.
Without question, something had gone south that day.

He found a whiskey tumbler and filled it with Jack Daniels.
Without ice. The whiskey was warm, sharp and bit his throat.
He emptied the tumbler in two gulps and repeated.

He then stumbled to his bedroom and into bed fully dressed.
He got into the fetal position and began sobbing.
Just like in his mother's womb.
That's where he longed to be right now.

Tomorrow, he will give a lecture to some post-docs
on the topics of Entanglement and String Theory.
He himself studied at the foot of Stephen Hawkins.

He thought he knew the nature of the universe and its laws.
He had worked out eloquent equations describing matter and gravity
in his university office. Published many notable papers.
His work was cited right and left.
Was thought to be one of the very few
who truly understood quantum physics.

But-- he was quick to castigate harshly those whose work
he deemed not at his level of intellectual distinction.
That habit was not endearing to the castigatees.
Powerful academic forces joined to knock him from his pedestal.
He was more fragile than imagined. At a faculty meeting this morning, he was
subjected to a final humiliation.
He fell from his perch and cracked like Humpty Dumpty.

Which brings us to tonight. He is a drunken, depressed mess
and even his status as a noble laureate offers no consolation.
As a theoretical physicist, he is good at thought experiments.
How about a scenario that ends in personal doom?
He is smart enough to know that is a distinct possibility.

Can he save himself? He is egregiously damaged but not fatally so.
Time-he'll be the first to tell you no one knows what it is-but
he knows like everyone else what time can do if indulged.

By the morning, he had committed to giving time a chance.
He went off to his lecture with a slight hang-over
and hope for redemption.

A GHAZAL DAY

My morning was filled with reading and reflection.
From the common journalist's fare to the great authors.

Damn the genocide in Christ's homeland.
Proportionality has been lost; the Old Testament God has returned.

My mind's eye sees crimson-colored children with shattered limbs.
"Nowhere to run, nowhere to hide" sang Martha & the Vandellas.

I turn from despair to quotidian matters.
I run/walk through beautiful scenery on perfumed grass.

Music rules the next part of my ghazal day. Notes, chords, scales, and modes
come alive on my piano, ukulele and guitar.

Poetry asserts itself much as hunger and thirst intrude into the day.
Its pangs must be satisfied though not all I consume is inspiring.

I attempt my own authorship though usually the results are
the least satisfactory part of my day.

But at day's end, I count nothing but blessings.
I have but to look at what I have.

POTPOURRI DAY

Famished for knowledge, love and greasy French fries
I went it alone; the crusty café and bar with
Harleys strewn in the parking lot
My waitress past mid-age but still meriting a leer
White synthetic uniform with auburn hair in a bun
And the name tag "Lola"
I ordered olives soaked in gin and fish 'n chips on paper
The relief from the gin coursing down my throat was immediate
I became gabby but no one was biting; I would dine alone
Just as Jefferson and Churchill had done many times
The fries were salted, scented, and satisfying-
Next came sorting myself out after my day
How can I describe a surreal day except with
Colors, images and metaphors
Like an Einstein thought experiment I had been riding a sine wave to
Determine my speed, spin and position
I ought to use more parataxis in my current writing I thought
And also read more Eastern medieval philosophers
Because Kant and Bishop Berkeley are falling short
I drank and ate to justify being in Dante's circle of hell for gluttons
I stumbled to the parking and lot and knocked over a Harley
Sometime later I awoke in the hospital
Courtesy of an indignant Hell's Angel

LIFE AND DEATH

A grand truth: We will all die
The minute we're born, we begin the march toward the end

Death should generate some curiosity
It's the only thing the living haven't tried

Yet the permanence of death makes us
Reluctant to embrace that level of commitment

We do want something good to take place afterwards
After all, we will be dead a lot longer than we'll be alive

But don't die until you become who you were meant to be
Then, when the crucial hour arrives, be not afraid
Not to be held by death, said St. Paul, was Jesus's triumph

A PROMISING DAY

Streaks of light emerge from the dark backdrop
Features of the earth's canvass reveal themselves
Moment by moment
A mountain, a lake, a valley, a gorge
Within minutes, our hemisphere is fully bathed in light
As our sun begins its arc across the sky
What will a day that has opened so promising bring?

RENEWAL

The morning freshness and calm after a heavy rain
Is uplifting for the soul and senses
Water drops teeter on dark green leaves
Brown puddles form haphazardly on the top soil
A crisp breeze nips all in its path

This is how the gods of nature provide renewal

WHAT I LIKE

I like Dante more than Didion
I find more wisdom in Psalms than in Proverbs
I delight in Falla more than in Fauré
I am soothed more by Khalo than by Kant
I am moved more by Tolstoy than by Turgenev

I like it better when wars end than when they begin
I will take the color azul over the color rojo
I enjoy conclusions more than premises
I favor questions more than answers
I am nourished more by irreverence than by orthodoxy

I prefer lonely lakes to crowded rivers
I will choose a frosty mountain peak over an ore-topped hill
I covet having a watchful conscience
I believe in Platonic forms over digital reality
I relish the unknowable between sunrise and sunset; and

I embrace the futility of writing poetry

What do you like?

AT A FUNERAL MASS FOR A YOUNG MAN

I sang the notes in the missal
From the hymn at page 433
My uncertain voice cushioned by the voices around me
The song's chords streamed from the organ
Floating across the aisles in comforting tones

The church-goers reminisced about the young man
-He had taken his own life-
Inexplicable to everyone but himself
Everyone knew he had so much to live for—
But this was not enough
Yet, we judge not where we have not walked in others' shoes

The eulogizers stood at the podium
With handkerchiefs poised
And told memorable stories about the young man
There was much to eulogize
Between the tears
The priest blessed the host
While the pious prepared to accept it
The young man once took the same host
In this very place from this very priest

The young man's own voice rang out
During the service
Singing from his heart a song from an album
At the crest of his musical career

The song told the mourners
That he had a musician's soul
And that music was at his core
Even as his guitar lay cold

I hope it is true
And he has found peace
"in a better place"
It's what he deserved

THOUGHT THIS EASTER

He rose after three days in the tomb
And said he would return soon
But it has been over two thousand years
Many full of sorrow and tears
When oh when will he return?
No time soon that I can discern

MUSIC

MUSIC SPEAKS TO ME

Music is simply vibrations in the air
that composers transform
into vibrant sonatas
effervescent trios
demure adagios and
piquant finales

Music speaks through many genres
from chant and Palestrina polyphony;
Chopin etudes;
Schubert lieder;
Mozart arias and
Beethoven sonatas to
the modernisms of Glass and Boulez

To soothe an agitated spirit
submit to the tranquility of evensong
psalms, hymns, holy sonnets
madrigals and motets

The language of music expresses itself
through violins sounding delicate vibrato;
Through the delicate timbres
of the harp and celeste

The tension evoked by dissonance
parallels everyday life;
the half-diminished chord
hungers for resolution
like the healing of a
ruptured relationship

Follow a stuttering trumpet amidst
syncopated passages
giving way to the silky tones of the violins
bringing back the clarity of the home key

A coda brings a satisfying conclusion
to what the notes and chords and rhythms
have said to me

FOR THE LOVE OF DOO-WOP

It was summertime at Coney Island
We had a President named "Jack"
It couldn't get any better for teens in a hot city
Barely eighteen and out with my future husband

The beach, the warm air and the music
The Dubs sang "Could This Be Magic"
A classic from the doo-wop era
I danced to the song in my boyfriend's strong embrace
Young, happy, and with the world before us

Fifty years later, I hear the song again
As we sit at our kitchen table
Lyrics spark the memories
As if we were there again
The air, the sounds, the tingling of love

But there are no more memories for my love
He doesn't remember what I remember
It's hard to force the word "dementia" out of my mouth
The thief that robs golden memories
Including my love's memory of me

And so I sit and absorb the verses as I cry
I can still feel his arms around me as we danced
To that doo-wop number
That summer day so long ago

LISTENING TO ELVIS

Elvis was a mama's boy
With a sultry, sensuous voice
Simple shimmering chords off rhythm guitar
And the rumble of bass
Provided spine-tingling intros for his songs

His rock-a-billy hits streamed across
AM stations
In the days when I played sandlot ball daily,
Fighting off the sweat and grime of
San Berdoo summers

He erupted like a volcano through the transistor radio
Sending a jolt up the spine
Fueling juvenile instincts

His music was provocative for the time
White man sounding black
White girls could pine for him
Without race getting in the way

His slow erotic songs stirred young hormones to a froth
With longing for the unattainable:
"One night with you is all I'm praying for"
He sang of love at all costs ("Treat me like a fool, treat me mean and cruel,
but love me")
Sang of hotels for the lovelorn
And about the pangs of Suspicious Minds

Some things didn't seem right:
Elvis from the waist up on Ed Sullivan
His backup group-the Jordanaires
The name too tepid to go with "Elvis the Pelvis"
And Vernon didn't seem like an apt name
For the father of The Pelvis

He was best was in the early years
When he was raw, thin and uncensored in spirit
Not so cool later on-- bloated, beaded and tasseled in Las Vegas

An Elvis song always sends me back to when I stood
Sweaty, grimy and happy with glove at the ready
In the oven of a San Berdoo July.

Elvis was an icon
And icons don't live out normal lives
His legacy will stand -not Graceland- but his music
Will Cobain and Jay Z endure like that?

OVER THE MOUNTAIN, ACROSS THE SEA

(A song by Johnnie and Joe from the Jim Crow Era)

This haunting song moved me at the age of eleven
Long before I discovered that "Johnnie" was female
Long before I learned the song's chord progression

A song about separation and longing
The lyrics were a cut above
the average song of teen romance in the '50s

The Johnnie and Joe duet alternated the verse and harmony
Weaving a marvelous mélange of sound

The song charted in 1957 during the ascendancy of early rock 'n roll
A time of open white racism
These singers could not stay at white-owned
establishments when performing in the South

The era is remembered as "simpler"
But only for whites
Secure in white privilege

The song puts me back in my eleven-year-old skin
During the hot San Berdoo summers in Okieville
Watching American Bandstand and the Mouseketeers on TV
Wishing I could be so lucky as to be a Mouseketeer
And sing and dance next to Annette
Luckier than Johnnie and Joe
In that hard era of Jim Crow

WHEN I LISTENED TO THE BEACH BOYS

In my teen days when I listened to the Beach Boys
I didn't know what lay ahead

Anything was possible
assuming I found the right path
'God Only Knows'

Would I attain success and luxury?
Or just tread water in life?

I figured 'I'm a real cool head'
But was that enough?

I drifted through the curves of those hot Berdoo summers
Lacking a guiding hand—
'Help Me Rhonda'

OVERHEARD AT A MUSICIAN'S FUNERAL

"He was working on his tenth composition"
"We all have to go sometime"
"It's just as well, I hear he was going deaf"
"I never heard his music, but someone told me it was good"
"He never got to conduct any of his works"
"How come the pastor didn't recite the 23rd Psalm I wonder?"
"His ex is not even here"
"I'm sure he didn't select the music at his funeral; just listen to it"
"They say he practiced so much, he got a little batty"
"Well, clearly the alcohol did its job"
"Glad it's not too cold outside today"
"What kind of food will they serve at the reception?"
"No, I didn't know him, I work in the cemetery office"
"Wonder who he's giving his grand piano to?"
"I hear his father was an alchy too"
"No, I didn't send flowers, they just get thrown away"
"Give my condolences to his daughter, I've got to run"
"His daughter ain't half bad"
"Give me a buzz"

POETRY IN LIFE

POETS AND MADNESS

I read Sexton and Plath this morning
Poetesses of disturbed brilliance

Join Plath in her obsession with father
Hear Sexton cry out in a psycho ward

They were both physical beauties with dark mental corridors
Their heads rarely turned toward the sun

In their poetry they coruscated pain,
galvanized brooding, painted dark images
and garlanded extreme states of anxiety

Male critics attacked Sexton's forward feminism
While Plath had her own struggles with a male poet

Anne and Sylvia did not live to be "full of days"
They shared suicide as an end game while still young

But they left the American literary canon richer
Dip into their oeuvre when you desire captivating word baths

BIRTH OF A POEM

Its gestation was not lengthy
Snippets of ideas swirled briefly in my mind
Before appearing on my laptop screen

I arranged and rearranged words and phrases,
Deleting, expunging, transposing, adding here and there
Trying to avoid cliché and forced metaphor

Reading aloud tested the metre and flow
Of my creation

Upon completion I pondered whether
To send this newborn into a world
Of harsh critics waiting to devour an imperfect creation

I was protective of my offspring
As any mother would be

After further editorial coddling and adjustment
I felt confident my offspring could survive any critics' slings
And perhaps provide pleasure for some reader

Venture forth little poem
Be optimistic that you will be treated well
Perhaps ending up in a respected anthology

I will now feed my progeny into Submittable
And remain hopeful

IS IT STILL A POEM IF NOT READ?

There is nothing sadder and more wasteful
Than poetry not read after its creation. Think of
The volumes stored away in attic boxes
Or sitting disconsolately on library shelve where no one goes
Dim, dusty stacks in every corner of the world holding
Poetry in a thousand languages, but forgotten by the ages

Is a poem still a poem if not read?
Or is it then only scrawled marks on a page?
Without meaning and purpose
Incapable of giving joy, pleasure or inspiration

Why then is poetry not always on display?
Featured in the light of day and on the broad avenues
So that those hungry for words perfectly cast can feast

We ought to be able to find a way to make poetry a daily necessity
After all,
We went to the moon
And found our way back

LOVERS AND WORDS

They made love
only through poetry

He would recite to her the most exquisite lines
in a most delicious way

Tender, erotic, brimming with passion
She could only be penetrated by his words

He was a virtuoso of the act, consummately skilled
She supremely fulfilled as a vessel of his words

She was most stimulated by sonnets, but madrigals could elicit
tingling in her fingertips, and terza rima made her moan

With each verbal thrust
she would cry in delight as his stanzas poured forth

They engaged their trysts in cafes and restaurants
or any other place that inspired the urge to read

The rest of the world fell away
as he opened his volume

The smoothness of his well-modulated voice provided foreplay
caresses came in light verse, kisses in velvety quatrains

The verses carried on his golden tones
inexorably led to a rapturous conclusion

He would read her poetry several times a day
She never refused a reading

POETRY IS NOT ENOUGH

Fallen into poverty,
I now live on the edge

Detested, degraded and
destabilized

I was once a two-car American
living the dream

Abruptly, I lost
my job,

My savings,
my home,

My car,
even my cat

I fought to keep my dignity
but poverty is as ravenous

as the black hole
at the center of our galaxy

My genus became
homo. homeless

Except for the pitying glance,
I am ignored by the more fortunate

When they see someone like me
they see an eyesore

They blanch and think:
"character weakness"

The sense of feeling like a person
deserving of a decent life evaporates
like morning vapors on the moor

Spiritual trauma accompanies
material losses
ABBA, why have you forsaken me?

PATIENCE

That of a leaf waiting for the win to transport it

Job waiting for the scourges to end

The sniper waiting for his target to come into view

The condemned inmate waiting for the final walk

The compulsive needing to watch the paint dry

Those waiting for understanding

The good waiting for their just reward

The prayerful waiting for an answer

THE INTERRUPTED POEM

The poet died quite suddenly
In the middle of writing a poem
Her heart just stopped pumping
As she reflected on a line break

What cruel force would
Deny a poet the pleasure
Of a finished poem?

The poem had begun beautifully
In flowing meter
And precise iambic form

The poem's subject was personal regret:
Never having had children;
Having ended a relationship with a devoted man;
Two novels with great promise abandoned
Before completion;
A decade lost to Oxycodone abuse

She had forgiven herself (just in time)
For decisions that seemed appropriate at the time
And for foibles whose only explanation is human imperfection

She had no friends
Who might finish her poem
Like the devotee
Who finished Mozart's "Requiem"

But on the 150th anniversary of her death
A descendant of the poet's brother
A music composer and poetry lover himself
Found the half-finished poem
Among others she had written
In a crumpled shoebox in the corner of a dusty attic

He resolved to learn more about his ancestor
But 22nd century search engines turned up no hits
About this poet relation
She had left no memoirs and
No one in the family had memorialized her life in any way

Not a single photo of her to be found
She had been a successful loner and recluse
The unfinished poem the only relic
And legacy of her life

The descendant resolved to
Honor her memory by completing the poem

He began by powdering her life's most prominent blemishes
He crafted justifications for her questionable life choices
She emerged in the poem as a self-sacrificing person
Who had done much good for humanity
And should be remembered for always putting
Others above herself

Alas, none of the lofty accolades were true
It was full-blown poetic license
Then again, a poem should never be constrained by reality
It transcends facts and life
And has its own edifice of values

The descendant used his skills as a composer
To set the text of the completed poem to music
In the form of a motet
One fine evening the piece
Premiered at the Tanglewood Music Festival
The music critic wrote in his review
That the piece "reflected a balance
of inspiration and melancholy"

Thus, our poetess lives on in text and song
It was more than she ever expected from life--
But that is the power of art

POETRY BLUES

No one likes poetry that I know
I say, no one likes poetry that I know
They say it's boring, hard to understand and so and so

But I like poetry, I'm here to say
Yes, I like poetry day or night
A poem can make me feel all right

It's the words you know
Yes, the words don't you know
They grab you like nothing else

If you don't like poetry
I say if you don't like poetry
You need to give it a chance

'Cause, listen, poetry ain't nothing but the blues
Yes, poetry ain't nothing but the blues
So don't matter whichever one you choose

TO THE CREATOR OF POETRY AND RAIN

I am awash in poetry this afternoon
As the rains cleanse everything outside my window

The rhythms and lilt of water and words
Lift my spirits as might a joyful 'Hallelujah'

All praise to the creator of poetry and rain
Whose sounds soothe me on this watery afternoon

TO MY FELLOW POET IN 2525

What a happenstance that you are reading these words
Penned by a poet (me) never known to the public
What kind of poetry do you write?
Lyrical, narrative?
What is "experimental" in your time?
Have Robert Frost and Walt Whitman stood the test of time?
I hope you have achieved your goals with poetry
Whether that be publishing or merely writing for yourself and friends
My advice? Never consider editors of poetry publications
as gatekeepers of the art.
Write on, write on, write on. We are poets.

Your fellow poet,
Augie Medina
April 24, 2021

THE DANGERS OF SLEEP

I penned a poem in my thoughts last night as I waited for sleep.
My piece was of soaring theme
crafted with words that would grip a reader's heart.

As I slipped into delicious sleep, the pieces started to fade away,
phrase by phrase, word by word.

Despite my fervent struggle to cling to the arrangement of words
on the tip of my memory
the dark swallowed my creation leaving not a morsel.

Not even the morning light
could restore what was mine last night.

HOW YOU KNOW YOU'RE NOT A POET

It's February already
I haven't written a poem all year
No motivation, no inspiration
Only frustration and consternation

No mental vapors to fuel even a solitary line

A real poet writes poetry all the time, real poets say
The real poet can't help it/can't explain it/can't explain it to me
She does it as natural as breathing

It gushes forth from pen or keyboard
Words in the best order with the right cadence
Correct intonation, right emotional edge—it's all there
When you're a poet

But when you're not a poet, the page remains blank
Bereft of the mind and heart's content

But I thought of John Cage's work "4'33"
This work is not in the mainstream musical repertoire
But it has some acclaim
If musical composition can be total silence
Why can't poetry be a total lack of words?

So here is my first poem of 2013
It is titled "Before the Big Bang"

....
....

....
....

Many readers will see nothing above
Until they give it a second read
And realize that it's only the first effort of the year
Of someone who's probably not a real poet

UP IS DOWN

The higher I went

The

D
E
E
P
E
R

I sank

Until I hit rock

B   O   T   T   O   M

And then I heard "clank!"

HUMBLED

One fiery L.A. winter day
with a July sun beating down in December
I strolled to the downtown public library
to peruse the scene

My technique is curious
I stare at volumes one by one, row by row, until
something attracts me and I pick it up

I wandered into the 'minor poets' section
The section is small
'Chicano Poetry' represented by a few volumes
alongside a volume of Folsom Prison inmate poems
next to an anthology of grade schooler poems

I pull the children's anthology and read
The poems take me aback
Imagination unleased—they are naturals
Describing home life in vivid images
Some lightness, some darkness, shades in between
They also tell of monsters and faraway places

Let us hope their future education doesn't destroy
Their natural poetic instincts
A truly humbling experience
To read the poetry of babes

ALBERT JOHNSON'S QUESTIONS

He titled his little volume
"Psalms for the New Millenium"
Published over a half-century ago
in free verse style modeled on the biblical psalter

Poems interwoven with fragments from Christian prayers
suffused with spiritual longing and homage
to the Judeo-Christian god

Al was concerned with who we are
Who He is
Where we come from
What our purpose is
Where we fit within science's explanations of the universe
Are we just wandering cells or something transcendent?
These were the big questions of Al's little book

Al's verses lament the strife among mankind
One poem about racial hatred was called "Color Blind"
Who knew about such a quality better than a blind poet?
Could he have imagined nine souls killed by racial hatred
during bible study half a century after he expressed hope
for universal brotherly love?

He repented for us all in his poem "Girl From Hiroshima"
Who were we to unleash atomic destruction in pursuit of victory?

I read Al's verses today and they vibrated with a prophet's
wisdom about man, suffering and the cosmos
suffused with hope for the future of mankind

I closed Al's volume thinking:
So long as it is not too late already

CHICANO/LATINO

THE JOLLY CHICANO POET:
FRANCISCO X. ALARCÓN REMEMBERED (d. 2016)

Larger than life
Both in girth and spirit

He lived his life as a poem
A poem without boundaries

Even his poetry book titles
Eran preciosos: <u>Mariposas Sin Fronteras</u>

He believed a poem was never complete
It took death to provide a final stanza
To his own poetic journey

A progenitor of much fine poetry
His verse landed on the page
Filtered through a Chicano lens

His style was eclectic
Using any form that conveyed
The content of his soul

His verse favored exploring Chicano culture
Mesoamerican history and Latino identity

Most of all, he was a progenitor of bilingual children's poetry
He proclaimed such poetry his crowning achievement

He thought children natural poets
And encouraged them to versify

Gay and married
He felt an outlier

Gay and Chicano
He had to tread lightly

But he approached life's dilemmas with doses of humor
Such as daily "thanking God" he was an atheist

On his death bed, he allowed his priest brother to give him last rites
"If you keep it short"
When his mother heard he had agreed to take communion
She exclaimed: "Does he know what he's eating?"

Let us nurture the glory of the Chicano poet, too few in number
Select a poem by the poet Alarcòn and shout it out to the world

Do this in remembrance of him

THE RADICAL CHICANO DOO-WOP SINGER

Rubén Funkahuatl Guevara
A man with his soul on fire
An icon in the East LA music scene
Since the start of rock and roll

Leader of Rubén and the Jets
A collaboration with Frank Zappa
A multi-racial doo-wop garage band
That knocked the socks off of local audiences

Women were always an obsession
As with a drug, sometimes he would overdose
He made no bones about his ever-present lust
Called it the "dog" inside him
Even into his seventies, he would practice his "moves" on the lovlies

Teacher, poet, theatrical performer
He was a repository of knowledge on Chicano popular music in LA
His signature song-poem was "C/S" [Con Safos]
Art was his life
He pushed the boundaries of performance art
On top of his vocalist core

He was never a household name
West of the LA River
But east across the 6th Street Bridge
He was a musical giant
He was officially named a Boyle Heights cultural treasure in 2012

But even his local fame and gigs
Never translated into more than
Subsistence-level living
On tour, staying in 5-star hotels
Back at "home" living in his car at times
He took it in stride; relationships and his art
Were the most important things in his life

Fire was a constant symbol and image in his life
He is still burning
Que viva Funkahuatl!

Based on Guevara's <u>Confessions of a Radical Chicano Doo-Wop Singer</u>
(Univ. of California Press 2018)

LATINX?

It seems that what to call ourselves has always been an issue-
We have been able to choose from a grab-bag of names

An entire lexicon has been created in this country
-for the most part, not by us-
in an effort to find an all-encompassing label

The Census folk have always been beside themselves
as to what name to use during their decennial count
We've even had the option of "White" or "Other"

Back in the day, it was easier.
There were only "Chicanos/Mexican-Americans"
("Raza" amongst ourselves)
concentrated in the Southwest
with the exception of the
self-styled "Spanish" "Hispanics" or "Hispanos"
of New Mexico

(In the interests of accuracy
only the uninformed
identify as "Spanish"
unless they are from Spain)

Later, populations like the
Boricuas, Dominicanos, and Cubanos
emerged as significant groups
outside the Southwest,
while Guatemaltecos, Hondureños,
Salvadoreños and Nicaragüenzos
replenished the southwest states and beyond

Over time "Latin American" or "Latino American" found favor
in mainstream use;
then "Latino" came into prominent use

BUT Latinx?

How did it ever come to this?
The thing is, "Latin" was inaccurate to begin with
But if we are to use "Latin" as a base
Better "o" than "x" as the extra letter

Por supuesto, I understand
The rationale behind adding the "x"
Gender-nuetral y todo eso
But sounding out the word "Latinx"
Feels awkward and uncomfortable in the mouth
Like it doesn't belong
And the word just looks wrong

Better to make up a
pleasant sounding name like
Mariposa or Quinto Sol
Por qué no?

PRETTY GIRL ON THE SONORAN SANDS:
A ROUTINE DAY AT THE BORDER

I have a friend who is a U.S. Border Patrol agent working along the Arizona border. One day, we were talking. I asked him about his day. He said it had been routine. His last chore of the day was to recover the body of a young female migrant who died on the desert sands on the U.S. side of the border. I asked how old she was. He told me she must have been in her 20s and very pretty. He described her teeth as very white and that she actually looked peaceful lying on her back despite probably having died of dehydration. That means essentially organ failure. How awful.

I asked whether she had any companions or possessions. No companions. Her possessions were scattered near her on the burning sand: a tattered cloth rosary, pink lip gloss, and an empty purse. No suitcase and no identification, so no name. My friend did the required paperwork on the recovery and clocked out.

My friend said the morgue would tag her as "Jane Doe." I thought, 'how sad.' How can she be nameless at the end of her life's journey? So I made up a name for her, Marisela. Why did I care? Well, I think every person deserves some dignity, even in an ignominious death. In my mind, Marisela was probably very smart, and with her looks, she could have been somebody here in the States. But she never got a chance to show her stuff—wasted talent, as they say.

I wonder about her family. Her next of kin can't be notified because she is forever anonymous. They will wonder why they never heard from her again. They probably don't have the means to try to find out what happened to her. They will carry an emptiness that will never be filled. What agony not to know.

Smart, pretty and with gleaming white teeth. What promise! My friend said, "No big deal. Happens every day." I was left wondering how the world can be so unbalanced.

CRISIS AT THE BORDER

The lovely flower-patterned cloth
covered the young man's body. He had
recently been with a Honduran human caravan

Hit by a truck
his bloody base cap rested by his side
his body straddled across a muddy road

The force of the impact had
knocked his right shoe off
revealing holes in his sock

He never intended to end up
in such an embarrassing position
he only wanted opportunity in a new place

AN ABUELITO AND HIS CRUCIFIX

December 14, 2016:
"Man, 73, fatally
shot by police had
crucifix, not gun."

An abuelito starting to decline mentally became fixated on his crucifix, which he had taken to mass for decades. Its symbolism meant so much to him, and it always had a comforting feel in his hands. One day he walked outside his home acting "a little strange." His crucifix flashed in the twilight. A neighbor envisaged a gun and called 911. The police units pulled up with guns at the ready. Alas, abuelito was not able to comply with commands to drop to his arthritic knees. As he raised the crucifix to the heavens like a priest does during Mass, he received what was later deemed a "justifiable police response." Twenty-three bullets tore into his chest. Medical attention arrived an hour later. The remnants of his crucifix were tagged as evidence. It seems that religion and violence have always drawn each other.

JACOB THE CHICANO WAR HERO AND DOTS

He was "just seventeen" (thanks Beatles)
But enlisted to defend his country in WWII
A country that didn't always treat its
Chicano soldiers with respect but
Jacob didn't think about that

He was shipped out to a remote Pacific island
In his very first combat, he became a KIA statistic
A Japanese bullet put an end to
The life of a barrio kid

Burials on the battlefield were hurried affairs
Jacob was buried in a foreign land
"With his boots on"
As the cliché goes

As in all tragedies
There are dots to connect
Starting with a small-framed Japanese
Female factory worker who examined
For quality control purposes
The very bullet that severed
Jacob's carotid artery
She fondled with her fingers that little piece of metal
Destined for Jacob
During inspection on the assembly line
And "passed" it

The other dot was the Japanese soldier
Coincidentally the same age as Jacob
Who aimed his rifle In Jacob's direction
Seeing an enemy helmet in his sights
He squeezed the trigger ever so gently
As he was trained to do
The bullet which had been examined
By the small-framed Japanese munitions worker
Exploded from the soldier's rifle barrel on a

Trajectory that found Jacob's neck

At the very moment that Jacob's 'ama
Was saying a prayer for him at Sunday mass
The bullet reached Jacob
Her prayer had been denied

The young Japanese soldier who took Jacob's life
Himself was killed the next month in another battle
Against "hostile forces"

The Japanese munitions worker
Who had inspected the bullet destined for Jacob
Visited the United States sixty years later as a tourist
While sight-seeing in downtown LA
She brushed elbows with one of Jacob's great nieces
On a crowded street in the jewelry district
Another connection of dots

With the help of modern DNA technology
Jacob's body was identified and brought home to rest
In Evergreen Cemetery
Another Chicano war hero

Jacob's great-niece
Visits his gravesite and wonders
What might have been

THE REPATRIATION OF AMERICAN ME

I was a mighty American soldier
A proud Marine schooled in death and destruction
Two tours of Iraq, three Purple Hearts, and a Silver Cross también

After the war, PTSD was my due
But I was fuerte and a chingón
What could anyone do to hurt me more?

Born in a little Mexican village three decades ago
My parents carried me across the Rio Grande
When I was eight
Brought up in Cali, I never realized I wasn't a citizen

I had proudly worn the uniform
Of the home of the brave and land of the free
Put my life out there for the good ole US of A
Pero no tenia "papeles" and ICE got scent of that
Via an employer whose "English Only" policy I had criticized
Steely-eyed ICE agents accosted me at the VA
Where I was going for PTSD treatments

Those desgraciados
Took me directly to the departure gate of the airport
No chance to say goodbye to wife and kids

To maximize the indignity of it all
They took selfies with their "catch"
Like fishermen with a prize Yellow Tail

I'm in an unfamiliar place now and
Though Mexican blood courses through my veins
The rhythm of life and culture are strange to me and I don't fit

I sought to assert myself as a true American
But the US Embassy turned me away
Where are all the "support our troops"
Countrymen that I fought for?

I have been disemboweled of country and identity
Leaving me adrift in unsettled foreign waters without rudder or sail

I was good enough as cannon fodder
In the only country I've ever known
And only fell short of the demands of an indifferent immigration law

But I will never abandon seeking the "life, liberty
and pursuit of happiness" I shed my blood for
It is my due
Semper Fi--it works both ways

MARISELA AND GOD

Once a proud school teacher
Until life became desperate
With more need than choice
She set her sights north
And challenged the lethal landscape
Of heat, cold, sagebrush and sand

Pink lip gloss
White socks
A tattered rosary and
Photos of loved ones
She carried these possessions
Along with her hope for a better life

These articles are now relics of her short life
Strewn across the Sonoran desert sands
Marking the terminus of her fatal expedition

Her name was Marisela
Now the Coroner's "Jane Doe"
Her face still pretty
Her teeth still white
Inside the orange locker room

There are those who will say that "she asked for it"
That she broke the law
"One less illegal alien" they exclaim

Guess they have a point
'Cause how could God Bless an America
With so many Mariselas?

WAR

MEMORIAL DAY MOMS AND DADS

The light dimmed forever in their eyes
The day the news arrived
They asked "Lord why?" Got no reply
They only knew
Their boy had died

On a field far away
His young life was taken
Gone a year less a day
His future forsaken

He'd been nothing but brave
When the round ripped his chest
Not yet meant for the grave
But he'd given his best

They said "time heals all"
But it just wasn't true
His loss cast a pall
Over all that they knew

Friends' tears finally dried
Not so Mom's and Dad's
They could never hide
Lives perpetually sad

They would forever wonder
Why their boy fell that day
To rend their lives asunder
But no one could say

Mom and Dad have now passed
Broken hearts was the cause
The pain gone at last
But leaving the loss

War eats sons and daughters
And wants more for the feast
Where's the next slaughter?
'Bring me more' says the beast

Let's try to starve war
Unleash peace, let it soar
So we can at last
Make Memorial Day parents
A thing of the past

THE IN COUNTRY BLUES

I saw my buddy cry in the rain and die
I cried too and asked 'Oh Lord why?'

Been humpin' in the bush for way too long
In a place where I don't belong

I near piss my pants when we get in a firefight
I ain't no hero, I feel like taking flight

Did I tell you how I felt the time my 16 jammed?
Excuse me Lord, but I said 'Motherfuck God-damned!'

Charley scares the shit out of me most at night
You really can't get 'em to just stand there and fight

Got plain sick first time I saw a man's belly ripped open
That it would never happen to me, that's all I was hoping

Back "in the world," Christ, they have no clue
But even if they knew, what good would it do you?

The other day my girl back home sent me a 'Dear John'
'Jodie' had replaced me and her love for me was gone

Man, I wanna go back to the world of the big PX
I need me some rock and roll and American sex

I won't tell my mom I been in so many hot LZs
I say to no one in particular 'get me outta here man please!'

Until you've seen a monsoon you ain't seen no kinda rain
The water just keeps comin' purt' near drives everyone insane
I miss my mom's cookin' man I really gotta say
'Cause them C-rats they are nasty, most of 'em anyway

Well I've been in the do-do where I felt my butthole pucker
Made me wish I was a rear echelon mother fucker

The other day I told my L T, 'sir I can't take this anymore'
He said 'PFC hang in there, I've heard all that before'

The day that I was wounded, felt like being kicked by a mule
And where I was hit, made me worry 'bout my jewels

Later at the hospital, a bald General strolled in and said
"Here's your Purple Heart, now get back out there for the win!'

Lookin' forward to a 'standdown'; choppers should be here today
Then again, the firebase is hot and dirty—it ain't no place to play

Jesus, if I make it back to "the world" I'll do anything you say
From then on, I'll be thankful for every single day

Then one day it hit me that I was 'short'
Started to imagine bein' back at a U.S. fort

One most excellent day, took my last ride outta the field
Got to that Freedom Bird, made it without being keeled

So that's my little song about the in country blues
Treat me right when I get home, 'cause you know I've paid my dues

HELP A VET

Born on the bayou in the late 40's
I grew up on country and hill-billy rock
My daddy was a dirt farmer
And I envied "Leave It To Beaver" as the ideal life

High school did little for me so
I jumped at Uncle Sam's invitation
to help contain the Red Menace in Vietnam:
"RA Drill Sergeant"

They made me a killing machine at Ft. Polk
and lost no time in shipping me off to Nam
so I could practice my skills

But stepping off that plane on arrival
-- feeling the blast of heat and smell of the place—
-and seeing all those body bags going home-
I truly wondered what I had done

I got past being an FNG
And learned the ways of the bush
Suffered the mosquitos and monsoons
And ham 'n egg C-rats

Day after day we humped after Charlie
And waited for our stand-downs
By now, I had no patriotic motives
Only to avoid KIA, MIA or WIA
Next to my name

One day, half-fried by the sun
sick with jungle fever
and just turned nineteen
I heard a chilling sound
A sound with pucker power

A mist streaked my face and chest
A mist that-- a split second before --had been two friends
That mist left me thoroughly fucked up
though I didn't have a scratch

After my year of boredom and terror
the Freedom Bird took me home

But it wasn't me
that arrived back in "the world"
I returned still ready for ambush patrol
But not for a normal person's life

I turned to beer and uppers and downers
They were my saviors until they weren't

I'd pace in my car with no sense of time
my demons as constant companions

At night, I'd feel wet from the spray of
my buddies exploding again
in my dreams

I tried marriage but that
ruined two lives instead of just one
Had two kids
but couldn't be a father because
I was weird from the war

My norm was biker bars, jail cells and stuff like that
Turned to Jesus once but my spiritual pain wouldn't budge
Tried PTSD therapy but it hurt worse than the disease

What happened to the promise of even just a regular life?
And other questions that I have

I now sit at an LA freeway exit
with white hair and resignation
Backpack stuffed with my worldly possessions
including my library card; I escape in books
Books don't promise and don't judge

My sign says "Help A Vet" but that's not likely
The country is full of "support the troops" braggarts
But it's more platitude than real effort

My one year in combat defined my life
That definition is dysfunction
My brothers misted by the RPGs that day in the Nam
were the lucky ones

I've lasted but not lived

I wanted to tell my story
in case you wonder
When you stare at me from your car window
And think whatever you think

CHILDREN

GRAMMAR SCHOOL GLOW

I see a halo around the elementary school
I hear the buzz of five-to-eight-year-olds
As they empty from the classrooms at day's end

The sounds of the children emit innocence and gaiety
I want to bottle this atmosphere for global distribution
The children hold the key to peace and sustainability

I relish their sounds
They provoke a smile and hope for us all
Let the children tell us how to live

VANISHED MEMORIES

My infant grandson Adrian rests his head on my shoulder
As we listen to soothing classical music
Programmed into his toy doggie, Giovanni

I don't know what Adrian is thinking
But we listen and enjoy

When I am gone, he will not remember these moments
No one knows where memories go for the departed
Those memories may vanish forever
But what sweet memories while they lasted

WALKING BY AN ELEMENTARY SCHOOL

Peals of laughter flood the playground
Hair waving in the wind
Running, jumping, spinning
The children poke each other in fun

I see the future in the schoolyard
Elementary school children, in their innocence
Malleable for the shaping of virtue and wisdom
We put a lot on the shoulders of teachers

I stare at the cuteness
That will eventually turn into seriousness
When they run the world
It starts out so charming

GRANDDAUGHTERS IN 2016

My granddaughters, Camila and Hana,
are fascinating to behold

To think they have-at two years of age-
The seeds of what they will eventually be

I see them in diapers and wonder
What will they look like in graduation gowns and wedding dresses?

Who will they choose to spend their lives with?
What will they remember about me?

Their choices in life
What would I say about their choices if I'm still here?

Dazzling creatures
Don't you know how curious your abuelo is?

Should I write them a letter they can read after I'm gone?
Explaining my curiosity about them when they were two?

STEEPED IN IMAGINATION

STEEPED IN IMAGINATION

In my imagination
I paint like Picasso

I am a lord of language
I write weighty tomes

As a violinist
I am without peer
Musical aficionados have wept
at my Mendelssohn

I can fall down mountain cliffs
and land as gentle as rain
If civil strife breaks out
I cannot be bothered

My lovers are faithful
All glad to receive my special gifts

I am on the verge of locating Noah's Ark
I say that without equivocation

I am also on the cusp of learning the secrets of black holes
and near to finalizing the mathematics of dark matter
Just the other day
the Event Horizon crossed my path

I am humbled that people every day
long for my awakening to enhance their lives

If I have any fault, it is that I
rely too much on my imagination
What if,
I am not who I think I am?

IN PRAISE OF THREES

Three strikes, you're out!
Fly balls, convictions, opportunities
Three pillars of truth and freedom

Three adages about friendship and loyalty
Three tales of anguish and despair
Three madrigals of love in the time of chivalry

Three authorities squarely on point
Three chest compressions
Three cracked ribs

Three curses of Ahab
Three trials of Job
Three sonnets by Bosie that set Urania ablaze

Three isles below the setting sun
Three colors of the rainbow
Three corners of the earth

Three persons of the Trinity
Three anathemas of Athanasius
Three condemnations of Arius

Three errors of the Nicene Creed
Three judgments of Paris
Three years of the Trojan War

Three misstatements of Homer
Three laments of Euripides
Three visions of Beatrice

Three passions of Paolo and Francesca
Three windmills that fell before Don Quixote
Three burnings of Helios

Three offerings of Aphrodite to Pan
Three years in Reading Gaol
Three days from De Profundis

Three bitter songs from Dies Irae
Three octaves above middle C
Three errors of rapture

Three punctuations forlorn in time
Three cubes of Picasso
Three paths of Swan's Way

Three sessions of sweet, silent thought
Three fragrances of Casablanca
Three odors of mistiness

Three lifetimes of laughter
Three moments forgotten
Three moments never lived

Three summits of Nandi Devi
Three meters to the abyss
Three minutes to eternity

Three sad moments of poetry
Three ways to end this outpouring
Three of everything

THE FERTILE MIND

Beauty that exists
only in a fertile mind
Your heroic actions on the day that never was
The novel of the century crafted in your dreams
Finding lost sonnets of Shakespeare,
the manuscript of Beethoven's 10th Symphony
and fragments of the poetry of Jesus Christ
A perfect rose
The annihilation of pride
A just society

WANDERLUST

When I think of all the places
I've never been
And that I'm certain
I'll never get to
I'm overwhelmed with wanderlust

Places near and far
High and low
Grand and picayune
Decadent and pure

Places of the past
Places that don't exist
All have in common
That I've never been there

But places of the future
Places in infinity
And at the end of the wormhole
I may yet get to

My wanderlust has hope

THE IONIAN SHORES

While dreaming of a pathway
Bound by rainbows and delight
I strayed onto
The Ionian shores of lore

There I saw
Haunting waves pounding black sands
Tangled eerie sunlight piercing foamy crimson water
And echoes of pain wafting into the frigid air

Some say Odysseus visited here on his way to Hades
But Homer mentions it not
Dido's lament was sounded here:
"Remember me, remember me, but ah!
Forget my fate"

The rivers Styx and Acheron pour into these shores
I expected to see Charon at any moment
Beckoning from his boat
For me to cross over with him

I did not stay long in view of
The intense stare of the Ionian shores
I thought it wiser to return to
More peaceful dreams

THE STRANGE DAYS OF COVID

THE DAYS OF COVID-19

People in masks, six feet apart
To stop the spread, that's the way you start

It didn't take long for this numbered contagion
To replicate itself and reach every nation

How can something so small cause so much destruction?
Spawning YouTube videos of hand-washing instruction

There's little about the virus of which we can be sure
But up to this point, we don't have a cure

We become apprehensive as the death toll rises
Go to work or stay home, which path is the wisest?

If you run out of luck and catch the disease
You'll soon be suffering from a cough and a wheeze

Chills, fever, headaches and joint pain
Inside all day and going insane

We hear new phrases such as "flatten the curve"
Stand in a grocery line if you have the nerve

We learn the meaning of exponential
And what sorts of commerce are deemed "essential"

Remote learning has put schools to the test
Lots of bumps and glitches, but they do their best

Alas, no more team sports on TV
Nor live concerts you'll be able to see

Working from home and meetings on Zoom
We try hard to resist any feelings of doom

Experts talk of models and herd immunity
Their advice to be heeded by every community

Scientists in government and in academe
In a feverish rush to find a vaccine

We cherish all those on the front line
Their effort and sacrifice truly shine

Give front liners all the protection they need
They risk it all, that's a fact indeed

When it will end is the question of the day
Keep the faith and be caring, is all I can say

A COVID-19 SONNET

It is the era of COVID-19
There is quarantine and isolation
People in clusters will not be seen
Its impact felt in every nation

The tiny culprit is a viral microbe
Its origin host a horseshoe bat
It unleashed a scene familiar to Job
Before striking, who knows how long it sat

The outbreak is labeled a pandemic
The virus spreads exponentially
Its scope wider than an epidemic
A stop to the spread we have yet to see

A vaccine will arrive in good fashion
Until then, exercise caring and compassion

DIRECTIVES FOR THE TIMES

Social distance your anxieties
Mask your questionable impulses
Scrub away your selfish inclinations
Quarantine your hurtful biases

But don't isolate your humanity
Let your empathy spread exponentially
Create a pandemic of love and caring
#Amor y Compasión-19

SOCIAL JUSTICE

LAMENTATION AND PLEA OF THE CHILDREN OF UVALDE

Let not our pleas go unheeded
For we have walked through the valley of death
We cowered in our classrooms, as other children had done before
The sounds of death ringing in our ears
Waiting for rescue, waiting for it to end

Between these ineffable events, grown-ups gnash their teeth
Wring their hands and offer thoughts and prayers
But these responses have done nothing to stop military-style
bullets from tearing our flesh and staining our classroom carpets red

Terror drenched Uvalde's Elementary School
The killer cut off all escape and
As we cowered before him
He coldly announced "It's time to die"

Then the rounds spit death from the frightful dark muzzle
At the same time that armed men in tactical gear
--Good guys with guns--
Stood outside our doomed classrooms in safety
As we begged for them to help us

We want every parent in America to imagine
His child in that situation of ultimate danger
Where death stalks the classroom
The very thought is hard to hold in the mind
Too dark and unfathomable

We are familiar with the aftermath rituals:
Prayers, condolences, grief counselors and flags at half-staff
Are followed by finger-pointing and acrimony
Between those in a position to stop these child massacres

Like waves crashing upon the shore,
There comes a lull between sets when all is quiet
Complacency reigns and the false serenity
Provided by elapsed time prevails

Then the waves start crashing again,
The sidewalk memorials sprout
And the cycle of treading water until
The next child extermination event begins anew

It is all too predictable- investigations galore by agencies
Of every type awash in probing what happened and why
Reports get completed replete with solemn conclusions
And well-meaning recommendations that will never be implemented

Hear us: we don't care why our killer-- not that many years older than us—
Emptied his high-capacity magazines into our tiny bodies
Because answering that question won't bring any of us back
And won't prevent the next mass shooter from having his own motive

The children of Uvalde, speaking for children everywhere,
Proclaim we don't care about blame
We just want to feel safe and be safe as we learn and develop

Are this country's schools not capable
Of providing safety for their children?
We don't think so, yet this country is failing:
Uvalde, Sandy Hook, Parkland, Stoneman Douglas,
And too many others.
Other countries do incomparably better—
Are we too proud to learn from them?

What will it take?
We protect the unborn; what about us?
Why have you forsaken us?

Even if there is no sure-fire way to stop these mass killers
At least make it harder for them
To get access to weapons that belong on battlefields
And not on civilian gun racks

We cry out to those responsible for protecting us
--Every adult--
DO SOMETHING!

GEORGE CRIED "MOMMA"

When the angry white man
Called young George the 'N' word
George cried "Momma"

When the security guard
Constantly dogged him in the store
George cried "Momma"

When the teacher said to George
College was probably not for him
George cried "Momma"

When the prospective employer
Asked him if he was a felon
George cried "Momma"

When the city librarian
Asked what he was doing in a library
George cried "Momma"

Each time the police stopped him on the street
Because he looked like 'someone we're looking for'
George cried "Momma"

With the assassin's knee
On the back of his neck
George cried "Momma" --
for the last time

Now, a nation cries for George
Why wasn't George heard before?
He had to die to gain respect?
George only wanted to feel
Like 'all men are created equal'
In the land he called his home

A HARD LIFE IN GEORGIA

She was 47 when she died
Her children—and even Pope Francis
pleaded for her life

Yet there was distinction attached to her demise
The first woman executed in Georgia in 70 years
The only woman on Georgia's Death Row

The woman executed 70 years ago
perhaps got a bullet from a firing squad
Or was hanged from the rafters
The records are silent on how
that state-sanctioned murder was carried out

This modern woman received an injection of Phenobarbital;
nothing too messy in keeping with
evolving standards of decency

According to a jury of her peers, she had goaded her lover
to kill her husband—certainly a method more direct
than simple divorce

Still and all, she sobbed at the end
expressing her love for her children
and belated sympathy for her husband's family

It was memorable as executions tend to be
She sang several verses of 'Amazing Grace' in a minor key
She took three final breaths of the stale air in the room
And then she was still

SPIRIT OF THE SECOND AMENDMENT

my happiness is trigger happiness
I love the feel of the wood, metal and plastic
in my hands;
rifle, handgun, shotgun;
the shape of ammo
the pointy tips, full metal jackets

tumbling rounds
hollow point rounds
chew up that tissue
tear muscle and bone
give a cavity bleed
make an artery gush
see what you done
som' gun

AR15, AK47, Uzzi
humongous clips
bump stocks too
wish I could get an M60
no bad guy would mess with me

don't dare try to take my guns
the 2d Amendment is my gospel
Jesus died on the cross for it
amen and lock and load

JESUS IN L.A.

I couldn't believe my eyes
But there He was
Jesus the Christos as he appeared
In 1st century Palestine
The stories of his ministry and the Passions
Learned from the catechism of my youth

The Second Coming? Here in L.A.?
"Why here, Lord?" His answer was that
His flock was here in abundance
The marginalized, the homeless, the demented and damned
The trivialized, vilified and demonized

"All well and good, Lord
But I have grave concern for you
The powers will not believe you"
He replied "nothing new there"

"My Father begot my destiny
Which I must pursue
Until all men understand"

But the modern-day Pontius Pilates
Did not give credence to Jesus being in L.A.
Forsooth, he did not look like the traditionally depicted
Fair-haired carpenter
He was instead brown and shaggy
So how were they to know?

He carried his good news downtown, chapter and verse
People stopped and stared until
He upset the flow of traffic in the streets
Church, Synagogue and Mosque-goers
Honked madly at this long-haired, bearded, swarthy man
These righteous ones cursed Jesus' presence in L.A. Yes,
Cursed Jesus in L.A.

Finally, the enforcers of the law came to restore order
No trial this time; not even an arraignment where charges are disclosed
When Jesus thought to present evidence of who he was
By showing them the still visible scar
Of that long-ago sword thrust in his side
He reached for his waistband…

That night local news stations broadcasted about quotidian goings-on
With nary a word about the poor soul shot dead downtown
Reaching for his waistband
Those who knew the truth said nothing
For they were afraid

RACISM'S CIRCLE OF HELL

In its most virulent forms
Racism is like piercing hot metal
That scalds the soul
Leaving a permanent stain
On those it touches

The experience of a racist incident
Never leaves the victim's memory
It festers in the mind and sometimes
Is regurgitated as dark remembrance

It can be subtle
Yet still recognizable
And inflicts harm even in its mildest forms

Those in the first circle start with a profession of
Denial of intent to offend
But the result is nonetheless a bulls-eye
To the heart of the target

A middle level in the Circle
Features those who would not directly inflict genocide
But who would tolerate such efforts

At the bottom of racism's circle of hell
Are those whose desire is extermination
Of non-whites and Jews
The teachings of eugenics imply a hierarchy of races
Learned students of this pseudo-science encompass
Hitler to today's Proud Boys
As well as the vermin who fester in the chat rooms of 8Chan

Racism is part of the eternal question of theodicy
How can a just god allow such a scourge to exist?
There are all the usual rejoinders such as "men have free will"
But that doesn't explain a compassionate, caring god
Just standing by
While People of Color and Jews
Suffer the slings of passionate hatred

ACKNOWLEDGMENTS

"Lady of the Books" and "Is It Still A Poem If Not Read?" were first published in the <u>Altadena Poetry Review Anthology 2019</u> (Shabda Press 2019)

"Fire Was Never Enough" was first published in Poetry Repairs: Contemporary International Poetry, Vol. 14, January 2014

"Tender Fingers of Night" was published in Poetry Repairs: Contemporary International Poetry, Vol. 14, April 2014

"Lovers and Words" and "Steeped in Imagination" were previously published in Poetry Repairs: Contemporary International Poetry #218, Vol. 15, November 2015

"The Ionian Shores" was first published in Poetry Repairs: Contemporary International Poetry #223, Vol. 16, April 2016

"In Praise of Threes" was published in <u>Stars in Our Hearts</u> (World Poetry Movement 2011)

"Marisela and God" was published in LatinoLA April 20, 2021

"Guanajuato Sunrise" was published in LatinoLA April 30, 2021

"George Cried 'Momma'" and "Pretty Girl on the Sonoran Sands: A Routine Day on the Border" were published in LatinoLA May 1, 2021

"Jacob the Chicano War Hero and Dots" was published in LatinoLA
    May 29, 2021

"The Jolly Chicano Poet: Francisco X. Alarcón (d.2016) Remembered"
    was published with the title "A Chicano Poet Remembered:
    Francisco X. Alarcón (d.2016)" in LatinoLA June 10, 2021

"The Jolly Chicano Poet: Francisco X. Alarcón (d.2016) Remembered"
    was published with the title "A Chicano Poet Remembered:
    Francisco X. Alarcón (d.2016)" in Somos Escrito 2023

"Latinx?" was published in LatinoLA July 10, 2021

"The Radical Chicano Doo-Wop Singer" was published in LatinoLA
    July 14, 2021

"Guanajuato Sunrise" and "George Cried 'Momma'" were published in
    La Bloga Literary Blog September 21, 2021 at
    https://labloga.blogspot.com/2021/09/small-piece-of-global-
    event-my-best-2.html and recorded as YouTube videos September
    2021 for La Bloga Literary Blog at
    https://youtu.be/2L_KgQPPs6k